RESULTS DON'T MATTER

RESULTS DON'T MATTER

How to Refocus Your Efforts on the Things that *Do* Matter

JIM VASCONCELLOS

San Diego, CA

Results Don't Matter

How to Refocus Your Efforts on the Things That Do Matter

Published by:

BOOMERANG CONCEPTS

Unattributed quotations are by Jim Vasconcellos.

Copyright ©2020 Jim Vasconcellos.
Printed in the United States of America
ISBN 978-0-9823489-9-4

1. Business   2. Leadership   3. Self-Help

For my family.

Thank you for keeping me focused on the things that *DO* matter.

CONTENTS

INTRODUCTION

We spend a LOT of our lives in the workplace. It can be a source of great satisfaction, rewards, and learning in our lives.

And yet, for many, it is our greatest source of misery and pain. I have felt this pain. My family members have experienced it. Friends have suffered through it, and some still do. And I know that you are familiar with it, as well. How do I know? Simple: because it happens to everyone.

So what makes one workplace feel so fulfilling and rewarding while another just sucks the life out of you?

The difference boils down to management. Managers have an almost sacred responsibility to lead and shape a culture in which people can succeed and the business can thrive.

This book is not about easy-to-learn, paint-by-numbers leadership techniques. Leadership is not easy.

You can't learn it by jumping on the next fad in management. Fads don't last, and the results don't stick. And there is no secret formula. Secrets are meant to be kept hidden—the very opposite of this book's intent.

For anyone seeking an easy way out, this book isn't it. You won't find in its pages the answers to your workplace problems. But it will start you asking the right *questions*. It is not for those unwilling to change themselves first. It is not a source of ammunition for those who are fond of saying, "See? I told you so." The uncomfortable truth is, improvement requires self-awareness. If you are not willing to make this depth of commitment, save yourself the cost of this book and the time you would have spent reading it. Just put it down and walk away. It's not for you.

Ah, but you didn't put it down! Since you're still reading, it means that you are willing to do the hard work and self-examination—or at least curious enough to take in what I have to say. That's a start, because that openness is the first quality it takes to be better and lead others to become better.

Many people are not willing to take this first step. Their view is, *it's not me; it's them.* The book's title alone is usually enough to put them off and make them scoff, and they will continue down the same well-trodden path to mediocrity. The thoughts that follow are a culmination of ideas, observations, and experiences that can put you on a better path, one that leads to real and lasting change.

For over twenty years, I've been speaking about personal leadership and management. Meeting participants from all across the United States, Canada, and Europe has allowed me to gather insights from people at many different levels across a broad spectrum of industries. It is what, more than anything else, shaped my perspective about what succeeds and what doesn't in the workplace. And I wrote this book so that all the noise does not mislead you, so you keep your focus on the things that matter.

Chapter One

GARY THE CHEF

Gary was head chef at a fine-dining restaurant in New Orleans. The establishment had an impeccable reputation for its food and ambience. Gary was committed to upholding this reputation from his kitchen. Nothing would get in his way.

Whether it was at prep time or when the doors opened for the nightly swarm of patrons, Gary was notorious for multitasking. That is, he could do two things at the same time: work and yell. You could hear Gary running the line. Literally. He would yell at the wait staff about orders, at his assistants about the prep work, at the dishwasher about the dishes. He would even yell at the pot scrubber about the cooking pans.

Oh, and the pot scrubber? That was me. I had applied to bus tables, but they needed a pot scrubber, so I took the job. I was fourteen. It was my first job outside of delivering newspapers and cutting lawns.

Every Thursday, Friday, and Saturday night, I scrubbed pots and pans. My workspace was behind Gary's line of commercial ovens and stoves. There were no windows, so it didn't have much light or ventilation. It would get stinking hot!

The entire back wall was lined with big, deep stainless-steel sinks that I would fill with steaming hot water and detergent. Gary taught me to work it like an assembly line. The beginning was where he would pile up the dirty pots and encrusted baking dishes. Once they cooled, I would scrape off the baked-on food and soak them in the first couple of sinks, then scrub them clean in the next couple. And finally, I would rinse and hang them up. It was an efficient process.

But when Gary got slammed with orders, he went into "multitask" mode. With no regard for our process, he would take hot cast-iron baking dishes out of the oven with tongs, come behind the stoves, and launch them directly into the suds-filled sink as he yelled at the wait staff, "You need to pick up your orders!" I would get splashed with hot, dirty, grimy water. And as I was standing there dripping, he would growl, "Hurry up and get these things cleaned!"

Being treated that way was intimidating. It made me feel small. It made what I was doing seem insignificant and unappreciated. It was frustrating, and it made me angry! I went into survival mode. I kept my head down, tuned out the noise, and did my job.

At that point, I didn't "want" to work for Gary. I "had" to. I began to search for a way out. I just wanted to get away from him. That day couldn't come fast enough.

Then one day, everything changed. The restaurant was shorthanded. Leo, the wait staff manager, called and asked me whether I was willing to be a busboy that evening. I jumped at the opportunity, although I admitted that I was nervous because I had never been in that role and didn't really know what to do.

Leo said, "No worries. You'll be fine. I'm going to be here to help and train you at the same time. Just show up in black shoes, black slacks, and a white shirt. I'll take care of the rest." When I arrived, he gave me a blue server's coat and black clip-on bow tie to complete my official uniform.

Leo laid out what was expected to create a pleasant fine-dining experience for every customer. Then he taught me what I needed to do in my role to provide that experience—everything from dining-room etiquette to setting tables, to servicing the customer, to supporting the wait staff. Leo not only made the role seem important, but he made *me* feel valued. I felt pride in what I was doing.

From that night forward, I stayed in that role. I was relieved that I didn't have to deal with Gary anymore. Unlike Gary, Leo was the kind of manager I "wanted," not "had," to work for. And I felt that way every single shift for the two years I worked with him.

What I Learned from Gary and Leo

Looking back, I do not doubt that both my managers were motivated to deliver a specific result. In this case, it was a fine-dining experience for the customer. Yet, from an employee's perspective, my experience with Gary was far from fine. I felt so beat up and drained that it took everything I had just to do what was necessary to keep my job. I began dreading going to work. With Leo, I looked forward to work. I wanted to do my best. I felt I was a significant part of what we were doing. It was energizing, uplifting, and inspiring.

We all have learned lessons from our work. My first was about the *impact* that managers have on people, workplace culture, and business. You may not see that you're doing it. You may not recognize how you're doing it. You may not even know when you're doing it. But you are doing it. This book is intended to raise your awareness of this, so you're not inadvertently contributing to the Gary Effect.

The Gary Effect

The "Garys" in management and leadership create toxic work environments—environments that take a heavy toll on people and are costly to a business. Yes, yelling is an obvious, easily recognizable poor behavior. For now, we will let it represent all the behaviors that do not provide positive, productive support for people to thrive in the workplace—the actions that exclude rather than include. There are numerous surveys and statistics related to this impact. Here is just a sampling:

- Half of American workers have quit their job to get away from a bad manager. (Gallup survey)
- Fifty-eight percent of those who left a job due to a toxic workplace culture claim that "people managers" are the main reason they ultimately

left. (Society for Human Resource Management)

- The cost of turnover due to workplace culture over the past five years is $223 billion. (2019 survey by Society of Human Resource Management)
- Seventy percent of the variance in employee engagement scores is due to managers. (Gallup survey)
- Only 13 percent of employees worldwide feel engaged at work. (Gallup survey)
- Sixty-one percent of bullies are bosses. (Workplace Bullying Institute)
- Workplace stress costs the economy around $300 billion per year in absenteeism, diminished productivity, and legal and medical fees. (American Institute of Stress)

Overwhelmingly, these statistics show that many managers are demoralizing employees and hurting their organizations' bottom line. While most people have experienced some form of this toxic situation, the leaders almost never see themselves as part of the problem that creates these statistics.

In the twenty-odd years I've been in the business of management and leadership development, I have yet to meet a manager who deliberately wants to make her or his subordinates miserable or sabotage their results. Not even Gary wanted that. (I'm not saying they're not out there; I'm just saying I haven't met them.)

So if it's not intentional, what is causing managers to respond in ways that lead to these sad statistics?

It's a matter of focus. In the career development process, everyone learns to *focus on results.* Here's how it happens:

Your organization hires you as an employee. You're given an objective. You do your job. If you produce the desired result, you are rewarded. You're given new opportunities for growth and visibility, and as you accomplish the desired results, you get pay increases and more responsibilities.

When you move into management, the process repeats itself, so you continue to do what you know. You focus on the results, and rightly so.

Focusing on *results* is seen as the key to success. It's such an easy measure of value, you don't have to think of anything else. The result is either bad or good, failure or success. Or something in between. But when results become more important than how you are getting them, expect repercussions, not just for you but also for those you lead. That's the Gary Effect.

Shifting Focus

The "Leos" in leadership are just as aware of what they need to achieve as the "Garys." They are aware of the need to produce. They are aware of the need to be recognized—not just for themselves but for those they lead. To accomplish this for everyone, they shift their focus from purely results to what is critical in getting the results: *their own actions.*

This is easy to say. But applying it is a little trickier, because it's not what we're used to doing. It takes hard work, but it is what serves everyone best. This creates a positive impact on employees, the workplace culture, and the business. And in the long run, it makes you more valuable and your job more rewarding.

Now let's rewind so we can better understand why it is so critical that we shift our focus. It comes down to a simple lie—a lie that is causing managers to focus on the wrong thing. We'll talk about that next.

Questions That Matter...

- Are any of the survey statistics we mentioned present in your workplace?

- Is it possible that you are inadvertently *contributing* to these statistics?

- Are poor behaviors being normalized in your environment?

- Are these behaviors affecting people's attitude?

- Have you noticed times when your behaviors are more Gary-like? More Leo-like? What is causing this shift between the two?

Chapter Two

THE LIE

You've been told over and over, in myriad ways, that *results are the thing that matters.* But it's a lie—one that you've heard throughout your life from business leaders, managers, teachers, professors, politicians, parents, and friends. You have heard it told in many ways: *Focus on results. Results are everything. Results are the only thing that matters.*

Such statements and their infinite variations don't work to get you what you want. Why? Because *you can't control results.* And just so you know, this is coming from a control freak.

All those statements—focus on results; results are everything; results are the only thing that matters—

contradict universal laws. Yet somehow, when it comes to getting what we want, we throw those laws aside; we ignore them. But the thing about laws is, they don't care whether you heed them or not. They just go right on having their same irrevocable effect on the universe—and on little old you within it.

The universal law that we have been ignoring is Newton's third law: For every action, there is an equal and opposite reaction. You can't have a reaction without an action, and results are nothing but a reaction.

CAUSE
Action
(Why It Happens)

➤

EFFECT
Reaction/Result
(What Happens)

And yet, each day, we focus on the result, not on the action.

We all struggle with this. You struggle with it. I struggle with it. Our colleagues and competitors struggle with it.

We struggle with it personally. Who hasn't said, "I need more money"? We've all been there. But money is merely a reaction to the act of learning more and earning more.

The Lie affects our kids as well. Teachers are told they need to bring up the test scores. But teachers don't raise scores. Kids learn. When kids learn, their test scores go up. Learning is a reaction to the approach, care, and environment that are provided for the children.

When teachers have the wrong focus, children learn the same faulty premise. Who, as a kid, hasn't been thankful for the person in the class who asked, *"Will that be on the test?"*? Again, we are focused on the result—that is, the grade. Give me that "A," and I'll be happy. We don't care about the learning, the competence, or the application.

It's why good parenting is so critical. We want our kids to grow up to be mature, responsible, self-sufficient, valuable contributors in the world. But that, too, is just a reaction. It's a reaction to the way that we as parents provide structure, establish boundaries, teach them right from wrong, and live our values daily as a model for them.

Everything going on in your life is a reaction to what you've done on the front end. The same premise applies in business, and it causes us to struggle professionally.

When we want to increase revenue, we tell salespeople, "Sell more." But we don't really *sell*. Rather, customers *buy*. Buying is a reaction to a salesperson adding value and communicating that added value in such a way that the customer sees the cost of the solution as less than the cost of the problem the customer is having.

When we want to increase the flow of customers through our business, we tell our customer service reps, "Make raving fans." We don't 'make' raving fans. We don't put them together like a puzzle. Customers return. Returning is a reaction to professional, high-quality service and assistance.

When we want our employees to be more productive, we raise their quotas. But productivity is not about quotas. Productivity is about performance. And performance is a reaction to the way you treat people—the way you support them, coach, mentor, and train them. It is a reaction to the way you include them—to the way you share information, ask for input, give recognition, show respect.

In business, we try desperately to manage the *result,* while the only thing we have control over is the *action.* Yet we continue to manage the result and pretend that our actions don't matter.

The French Enlightenment writer and philosopher Voltaire said that words like *luck, chance,* and *coincidence* were invented to express the known effects of the unknown causes. In other words, if you focus on results rather than on your actions, you are leaving the success of your relationships, your career, your business, and your *life* to happenstance. Managers can't afford to leave their success and the success of those they lead to chance. The effects can be devastating.

By having us focus on results, the Lie is pushing us further away from the things we want. As you will see in the following chapters, the Lie takes a huge toll on human capital and a company's bottom line.

Ironically, I'm going to show you why **results don't matter** and how to leverage this surprising truth to get *better* results.

Chapter Three

THE CONSEQUENCES OF PUTTING RESULTS FIRST

When the result becomes more important than your actions, poor choices will inevitably follow. It applies to everyone—every role, every job, in every business in every industry. That's the thing about a universal law—there are no exceptions.

Take boxing, for example. When professional fighters land that first big punch that hurts their opponent, some get greedy and try to land another, knock out their opponent, and win the fight.

But fixating on that result causes the fighter to lose sight of the things that matter—the things that created the opportunity for that good shot in the first place. So they leave themselves unprotected, allowing the opponent to come back with the knockout punch. And what looked like a win for the result-fixated fighter ends in defeat.

Managers who have their eyes exclusively on the prize will eventually suffer defeat as well, because they have lost sight of the actions that support and guide their workforce.

THE LIE...
RESULTS ARE THE ONLY THING THAT MATTERS.

This misconception is so common, it has resulted in an *epidemic of mismanagement.* Just ask any worker in an organization. They'll tell you all about how this or that manager has pressured them, blamed them for mistakes, taken out frustrations on them, taken credit for their work or ideas, excluded them, berated and intimidated them, faulted others for lack of communication, given unclear direction, and even retaliated against them. And if you talk to the managers, they'll tell you the same thing about *their* managers.

Managers blame employees. Employees blame managers. Managers blame other managers. The buck never stops.

This dynamic creates a toxic environment. The culture begins to erode. Trust breaks down. Confidence crumbles. Relationships wither. Opportunities go begging. Morale declines, and performance suffers.

As long as you continue to buy into the Lie that *results are the only thing that matters*, the things you want will slip further away from you.

Theranos

Elizabeth Holmes, CEO of Theranos, was determined to create a machine that could accurately diagnose multiple health conditions from a single drop of blood. That meant no hypodermic needles for venous blood draws. You would be able to go to a walk-in clinic and, with a simple pinprick of your finger, get a full range of blood tests. No labs needed! Her machine would revolutionize blood testing and change the healthcare industry.

Theranos employees were excited. They knew what it meant to be part of this—they were in on something huge. They were ready and willing to rise to the challenge.

Along the way, they ran into problems developing the technology. Some expressed concern with the feasibility of the project's parameters. Some voiced concerns over quality control. Some cautiously articulated ethical issues. Leadership viewed this input as resistance—even disloyalty to the cause. This "naysaying" attitude put the desired result in jeopardy, and any doubters were treated as untrustworthy.

A reporter named John Carreyrou originally investigated Theranos's claims. He wrote a book about it, titled *Bad Blood*. In it, he said, "Employees who would try to raise questions were either fired, or marginalized, or left of their own volition."

Despite repeated warnings from employees that the machine wasn't ready to go live on human subjects, Holmes remained fixated on the result.

Ignoring the unwelcome input, Holmes put the machine out anyway. The result was a disaster. Samples were stored at incorrect temperatures. Patients got faulty results. The people who called Theranos to complain were ignored. Ultimately, nearly a million tests conducted in California and Arizona had to be voided or corrected. Holmes was ousted as Theranos's CEO and is facing jail time for fraud.

So let me repeat myself: *as long as you continue to buy into the Lie that results are the only thing that matters, the things you want will slip ever further away from you.*

A "Yes" Culture

In their eagerness to deliver, result-fixated managers use poor leadership techniques. They ...

- ignore input,
- dismiss alternatives,
- marginalize differing perspectives,
- favor conformity,
- disregard questions,
- force compliance,
- fail to guide,
- demand,
- threaten,
- demean,
- micromanage.

These actions force a "yes" culture, in which people are wary, reluctant, or just plain scared to speak up. This sort of toxic culture tends to arise whenever *results are the only thing that matters.*

The unspoken message is clear enough: deliver without question. If someone expresses an opinion, suggests an alternative direction, questions a decision, requests help, or points out a flaw, they are met with a "results are all that matters" type of response: "Just do whatever it takes" … "You're not being a team player" … "If you can't do it, I'll get someone who can."

Such responses, implied or overt, threaten a person's security. They become concerned with repercussions. Questions loom regarding how they will be perceived. *Will this affect my career, reputation, image, or credibility? Will it hurt my chances of a promotion, raise, or future opportunities?*

Whether by design or by default, that's how a "yes" culture gets created. Candid perspectives, honest insights, and direct opinions get quashed or sidelined.

When people can't be up front and candid with their managers, they tell the manager what the manager *wants* to hear, not what she *needs* to hear.

As the manager, it's tough to get the result you want when you have only a partial view of the issues. Your perspective will be based on …

- half-truths,
- misleading information,

- overinflated capacities to deliver,
- impractical timelines,
- and false impressions.

Then the epidemic of mismanagement continues. It causes you to …

- make unrealistic delivery promises,
- develop faulty goals,
- create unrealistic expectations,
- set unfeasible timelines,
- and confuse priorities.

Employees then …

- get overwhelmed,
- feel frustrated,
- waste resources on lesser priorities,
- waste time,
- lose confidence,
- have morale issues,
- and generally get stressed!

With all this internal turmoil, sooner or later, the overpromising and underdelivering starts to affect your customers. Some customers take the time to tell you what you can do better, by making a complaint. But most won't bother. They just quietly take their business elsewhere.

And it's all a result of thinking that *results are the only thing that matters*. Like the fighter, you become so focused on the result, you lose sight of what's important to achieving that result. It's why you end up further away from what you want.

Doug Conant, former CEO of Campbell's Soup, said, "To win in the marketplace, we must first win in the workplace." Conant understood that he would not achieve the results he was hoping for without cultivating the success of all the employees.

Chapter Four

THE HIDDEN COSTS OF PUTTING RESULTS FIRST

Thinking that *results are the only thing that matters* is the contagion that has spread this epidemic of mismanagement. This mind-set is costly to a business, its employees, and its customers. Sometimes, it's a tangible cost such as money, stock price, or employee turnover. Sometimes, the cost is subtler: strained relations, a tarnished image, poor employee health.

When you decide to circumvent universal laws and manage the result instead of your actions, you can be sure there will be a cost. Here are some examples.

Lost Dollars and "Sense"

This first self-inflicted fiasco happened at the major financial institution Wells Fargo. Leadership wanted to increase revenue, so they increased the product sales quotas for their retail banks.

Managers then pressured employees to open more accounts. Some managers used questionable tactics. Some told their subordinates to "do whatever it takes." Now, that's a pithy motivational line in a movie script, but in the real world, it is apt to start the company down a slippery slope.

Here's the proof: Employees followed the order and did whatever it took, opening over three and a half *million* deposit and credit-card accounts! Impressive results, but the accounts were all opened *without the customer's consent*!

So for starters, Wells Fargo got hit with $185 million in fines. And the company racked up huge legal costs beyond that. Down the line, it made a $575 million settlement with the various states where the fraud occurred. The company's reputation took a major hit, losing the trust of its customers. And the almost daily bad headlines hurt its credibility with the public—all potential customers.

Thinking that *results are the only thing that matters* leads businesses, managers, and leaders to waste staggering amounts of time focused on the wrong things. And when your focus is off, you end up *mis*leading—not only yourself but the people around you.

That's why it's a lie. That's why it doesn't work to get us what we want. And that's why there's a hefty price to pay every time you fall for it.

Wrecked Reputation and Tarnished Image

This next example began with the employees of United Airlines. Gate agents had to get four of their crew members from Chicago to Louisville for another flight they needed to serve. The Chicago flight was full and already boarded. United agents offered compensation up to a thousand dollars to any customer willing to give up their seat. No one accepted the offer.

The gate agent then picked four passengers, supposedly at random, to remove from the flight. Three left the plane without incident. The fourth passenger refused to give up his seat, saying he was a doctor and had to get home to care for patients.

Employees called airport security. Security arrived and forcibly pulled the fourth passenger from his seat and dragged him off the plane, in the process giving him a concussion, breaking his nose, and knocking out several teeth. The four United employees were then allowed to board. Result achieved!

Oh, but it doesn't end there. When you focus on the wrong things, there's always more to come.

The event didn't happen in isolation. It went down in a plane full of customers who were recording everything on their phones. They immediately posted the videos on social media, where they quickly went viral. The cost escalated.

All the major news networks played the videos incessantly, creating a public relations nightmare. United's image took a crippling blow. Customers began to rethink their loyalty, and investors got a backlash as the stock value took a $900 million dive. The fourth passenger filed a lawsuit for pain and suffering and received a settlement of $140 million.

I hope the result was worth all that. (And yes, that was sarcasm.)

Sacrificed Integrity, Principles, and Values

There are also scenarios in which the focus on results affects our children. Forever etched in my mind is the Atlanta Public Schools cheating scandal.

In 2002, my children were in elementary school in Georgia. That's when President George W. Bush enacted his education plan called No Child Left Behind. With this plan, to receive federal funding, the states had to develop and administer standardized tests to measure improvement. The drive continued in 2009 with President Obama's education initiative called Race to the Top. This program would have states competing against each other for federal funds, based on scores.

Here's how the Atlanta Public Schools (APS) implemented the program that led to the cheating scandal. The following excerpts are from the indictment published in the *Washington Post* in 2015:

> While Superintendent of APS, Beverly Hall set annual performance objectives for APS and the individual schools within it, commonly referred to as "targets." If a school achieved 70% or more of its targets, all employees of the

school received a bonus. Additionally, if certain system-wide targets were achieved, Beverly Hall herself received a substantial bonus. Targets for elementary and middle schools were largely based on students' performance on the Criterion Referenced Competency Test, a standardized test given annually to elementary and middle school students in Georgia ...

The Georgia Department of Education requires that the CRCT be administered under conditions to prevent tampering and other irregularities that could affect test results. Any deviations from these procedures are prohibited. Beverly Hall was required, by statute, to abide by and enforce the regulations of the regarding test administration and to certify in writing that those regulations had been followed.

APS principals and teachers were frequently told by Beverly Hall and her subordinates that excuses for not meeting targets would not be tolerated. When principals and teachers could not reach their targets, their performance was criticized, their jobs were threatened and some were terminated. Over time, the unreasonable pressure to meet annual APS targets led some employees to cheat on the CRCT. The refusal of Beverly Hall and her top administrators to accept anything other than satisfying targets created an environment where achieving the desired end result was more important than the students' education ...

That last line is especially sad. It's hard to imagine administrators, teachers, and principals changing answers to improve the students' standardized test scores. When a result becomes more important than the actions taken to achieve it, people will begin to sacrifice their integrity, principles, and values. These same issues affect the relationships between managers and employees daily.

Lost Credibility, Damaged Relationships, and Broken Trust

In a manager's quest for results, you may be surprised—or not—at how common it is for a manager to "steal" an idea from a subordinate. I say "steal" because they take the idea and present it as their own. The individual or team who came up with it gets no credit.

Isabella D., an employee of a social media marketing firm, shared this story with me:

> I worked for a manager who frequently presented my ideas as his own. Before meeting with a client, I would have an in-house meeting with my manager to prepare for my presentation to my client. That's when I would share my research, work, and plan I designed. It was protocol to have a manager present during the client meeting. The problem is that my manager would interject and start to take over, using the information I presented to him in the premeeting. When the client showered him with praise, he would say, *I thought you'd like that.* He didn't acknowledge or give credit to me for anything. He willingly accepted the accolades for my work as his own.

It's my job to come up with ideas and plans for my clients. It's also my job to maintain and build an ongoing relationship with my client. I rely on my work to build my image, credibility, reliability, and trust with a client. That's difficult to do when my manager steals my ideas to boost his image.

While this manager may have built his credibility with the client, he lost all credibility and trust with Isabella.

Behavioral Blindness

The term "behaviorally blind" is used to describe those who cannot see how their actions are affecting others.

While I was shopping with my wife at a retail clothing store, this became obvious. As one sales associate was helping my wife, another came out of nowhere and asked my wife whether she would be interested in opening an account with them, saying she would receive 25 percent off her purchase.

You may think, what's so bad about that? Well, first of all, my wife was in the middle of trying on clothes. Second, she had made no decision yet to buy anything. And finally, the second sales associate just interrupted the customer while a coworker was servicing her. It was disrespectful to all of us, and it lacked professionalism and common courtesy.

BEHAVIORALLY BLIND... THOSE WHO CANNOT SEE HOW THEIR ACTIONS ARE AFFECTING OTHERS.

Since we knew the sales associate, we asked why her colleague had so rudely interrupted us. She said the manager had recently held a meeting and told everyone that the company was implementing a sales initiative for opening credit-card accounts. The number of hours an associate was scheduled to work would be reflected by the number of accounts opened. The highest sellers would be scheduled for more hours, and the lowest sellers would receive fewer hours.

Would the manager meet the target? Possibly. But at what cost? Poor service? Increased complaints? Strained employee relationships? Loss of business? Lost loyalty of both employees and customers?

To avoid losing their hours, employees were undercutting their team members by hawking to already engaged customers, as had happened with us. Employees would also manipulate customers to meet the directive. They would tell the customer to open the account for the discount, and then they could close the account later.

As a customer, I want high-quality, professional service, and assistance. Provide that, and I'll consider buying from you. Try to sell me before you help me solve my problem, and you've crossed a line. You haven't earned the right to ask for my business. I'll walk away; I have plenty of choices. All of us do.

Corroded Culture

When a manager focuses on the wrong things, it takes a toll on the workplace culture and the employees.

Here's how it starts. Managers hire an employee. They onboard him by laying out the expectations of what it means to be an "ideal" employee: things like being a team player, taking initiative, and "doing whatever it takes" to get the job done.

The employee is enthusiastic and begins with a sense of commitment to succeed. He is ambitious, determined, motivated. To make a good impression, the employee works through his lunchtime and breaks, even stays late to power through and be the "ideal" employee.

Does the manager notice? No. She sees only the results. So she adds to the workload. She even sends him emails and texts after hours. She has now passed the "contagion" on to her subordinates.

The employee struggles to keep up with the demand. In his haste to deliver the results, he makes decisions that mask his inability to keep up with his boss's unreasonable expectations.

The employee begins to sacrifice even more of his time by taking work home with him. He forgoes family time and vacation time. He even powers through when he has the flu. His frustration grows along with the stress as his morale drops. He becomes resentful.

"Do whatever it takes" takes on a new meaning. Self-preservation sets in, and the employee cuts corners to keep his job. Errors increase, and quality suffers.

It becomes a corrosive culture, detrimental to the success of both the manager and the employee, and to the overall health of the organization.

Remember, "results thinking" is a contagion. The more that people hear and can see that results are the only thing that matters, the more they become fixated on the result. It's a chain reaction that spreads like wildfire. No one is immune. Everyone is susceptible: leaders, managers, employees.

Questions That Matter...

- What is the premise that *"results are the only thing that matters"* costing your company?

- What price are you paying personally?

- In what way might you be spreading this epidemic?

Chapter Five

THE TRUTH

So what really matters?

Your *actions* matter. This is the plain and simple Truth that gets buried in the Lie.

The Truth stems from the universal law of action and reaction, cause and effect. No result exists until you have taken an action—anything that happens before that is pure happenstance. It's always actions before results. That's the natural order; you can't change it.

But that doesn't keep people from trying. Some people fight this law. They use their authority to *demand* results. They believe that power is what drives results. They think that if they shout loud enough or pound the table long enough, the desired results will appear—only to find that there is a heavy cost.

Some people choose to ignore the law rather than fight it. They try to get what they want through strength of will. They feel that if they put their head down and focus on the result hard enough and long enough, it will manifest. And they, too, pay a cost.

Some believe they can circumvent the law. They try to "outwit" the law. They cut corners to ease the pain involved in getting the result. When they fall short, they seem genuinely shocked—even more so when they get hit with additional repercussions for trying to get around the law.

But many more people are simply unaware. They don't know that they are not following this universal law. They unwittingly take the approach of the usual influences from their environment—the demanders, the willers, and the outwitters—and focus on the result. And as the result slips further away, they wonder, *Why does this keep happening?*

Whether through deliberate denial or just lack of awareness, you do not have to follow the law of cause and effect—you just have to live with the consequences of *not* following it.

It's a universal law, like gravity. You don't get to ignore it and walk away unscathed. There is a built-in penalty system, no judge or jury required. You and those you lead will pay the cost of not heeding it.

The Shift

Now that you've become aware of the destructive costs of focusing on the result, it's time to shift your focus to *your* actions. Now, of course I know that you know that actions matter. But the demanders, willers, and outwitters will distract you from taking the right course of action. They will pressure you to follow their lead and place all your emphasis on the result. This is not because of some nefarious motive to set you up for failure. It's simply because going for results above all else is really all they know.

THE TRUTH... WE DON'T CONTROL RESULTS. WE ONLY CONTROL OUR ACTIONS.

You must lead yourself first. Don't blindly follow their lead—*take* the lead! Self-leadership means you intend to improve your current circumstances through your actions. But understand that when you decide to take the lead, you will still face pressure to deliver, which is as it should be anytime you accept this responsibility. This generates a positive dynamic that will move you forward on this journey.

You will feel the pressure to meet self-imposed expectations. These may include securing your job, taking the next step in your career, being a leader in your community, supporting your family, maintaining your image, upholding your reputation, or being a positive role model for your children. Whatever they are, they will involve what is important to you.

You will also feel the pressure to help others meet the expectations you have proposed for them. By taking the lead, you have asked people to join you on the journey. You have committed to guide and support them toward success. You have promised, in so many words or implicitly, to reward them for their efforts. You have promised them an opportunity for growth. You have promised to help them fulfill their aspirations, and you have promised that the journey will add value to their careers and their lives.

Your actions, not intended results, are catalysts that foster growth, perspective, and drive on a journey that is not for the faint of heart. It will involve more risk than you expect. It will take more effort than you expect. But these are *positive* pressures.

As you shift your focus to your actions, you will feel the pressure to focus on results. That is a negative pressure. It's the Lie rearing its ugly head once more. Its message will be carried through the demanders, willers, outwitters, and, yes, the well intentioned but unaware.

If you become indifferent and give up, you will follow the lead of the demanders, willers, and outwitters. Results will be the only thing that matters to you, and you will break the commitments and promises that you've made. So don't lose focus. Don't panic. Don't become indifferent and give up. Stay focused on what really matters, by fulfilling the commitments and promises that you have made to yourself and others.

Living up to your commitments requires that you shift your focus to the actions that serve both the organization and your people within it. You will have to break old habits and form new ones. You'll have to develop a new mind-set. This is self-leadership, and doing it well requires discipline.

As you shift your focus to your actions, you will become more effective personally, and this will lead you to become the kind of person people *want* to work for.

The Truth about Performance

People perform much better for a leader they *want* to work for than for someone they *have* to work for. I worked harder and more competently for Leo than I ever had for Gary. And so will the people who work for you.

So what makes a person want to perform better?

To answer the question, let's step back and look at performance. Technically, performance (P) is the result of the application of a person's knowledge (K), skills (S), and experience (X). It's formulaic:

$$P = K + S + X$$

Theoretically, the more knowledge a person possesses, the more developed their skills are; and the more experience they have, the better their performance will be. But just because a person has the knowledge, skills, and experience doesn't mean they will apply these to the full extent they are capable of.

This means that performance is *at will*. People can turn it up, and they can dial it down.

So knowledge (K), skills (S), and experience (X) are the core elements of performance. But it is a person's effort (E) and willingness (W) that exponentially raise the *quality* of their performance (QP).

$$QP = (K + S + X)^{E+W}$$

This matters because the degree of effort and willingness a person puts out is directly proportional to the *quality* of the leader's *actions*.

And therein lies the answer to the question, *What makes a person want to perform better?* Answer: the quality of the actions taken by their leader.

A leader's actions can motivate a person to perform at their full capability. Or the same leader's actions can cause a person to do only what is necessary to keep their job.

Let's be clear. Your actions can cause failing performance. Your actions can cause mediocre performance. Your actions can cause "good enough" performance. And your actions can cause outstanding performance.

Shifting your focus to *your own actions* is crucial to improving the overall performance and effectiveness of you, your team, and your organization.

Actions, Not Vision

Notice that I didn't say your *vision* or *mission statement* is what improves the team's overall performance and effectiveness.

When I ask people to tell me what their organization's vision or mission statement is, they generally have to look it up on their company's web site. Such statements let you know the purpose of the company, but they aren't driving the quality of the performance. That comes from the leader.

When I ask people to tell me what impedes their performance at work, they rattle off a list of things their leaders do, such as …

- demand results without giving any clear direction why or how;
- intimidate;
- take credit for their subordinates' work;
- micromanage;
- ignore their subordinates' input;
- lack transparency;
- break promises;
- condescend;

- punish mistakes;
- don't trust the team.

This is by no means an exhaustive list—just a sampling of common statements. I'm sure you could add more from your own experiences. But these are all clear signs of the fallacy that *results are the only thing that matters.*

When I ask people what motivates them to excel at work, they mention a very different sort of actions by their leaders:

- laying out expectations,
- giving honest feedback,
- asking for input,
- providing material and moral support,
- addressing issues that impede performance,
- trusting subordinates,
- acknowledging superior performance,
- encouraging individual development.

When you shift your focus to what matters, you will see better performance, experience better interactions, build better relationships, develop better collaborations, and deliver better service. All these actions lead to better outcomes. And isn't that what everyone wants?

Okay, I get it ... but now what?

It's time to shift your mind-set to the things that *do* matter.

If you want to be a better leader, be more effective personally, and build a stronger workplace culture, you need to master three key components:

- Raising Your Awareness (Chapter 6)
- Identifying Actions (Chapter 7)
- Assessing and Adjusting (Chapter 8)

Well, don't stop now. Read on!

Chapter Six

RAISING YOUR
AWARENESS

It's going to take some effort to get your thinking right on this. It's been ingrained in us to focus on results. But remember what the law of cause and effect tells us.

CAUSE
Action
(Why It Happens)

→

EFFECT
Reaction/Result
(What Happens)

Anytime we try to fight this by managing the result and not our actions, we are *working backward*. We're focusing on the result and hoping that the universe—team, company, customers, friends, spouse, the government—does something to produce what we want. It happens in every aspect of our lives. We just don't see the mechanism for *how* it happens, and this leads to great frustration.

Road Trip

When my kids were young, my wife and I would take them on road trips to see their grandparents. The drive was anywhere from eight to twelve hours long. My intended result was to get there quickly and efficiently—the fastest route with the fewest stops.

It all started with packing. Whether it was for a weekend or a week, there was still the same amount of baggage—a lot!

I would tell my family to pack everything they wanted to take, and drop it behind the van, and I would load it. The pile always looked as if we were not vacationing, but *moving!*

I'd look at the pile, and then I'd look at the space I had to pack it into. Look at the pile. Look at the space. Each item was a puzzle piece. All I had to do was to find where each fit perfectly to maximize the amount of stuff that could fit into the given space. I would rearrange, squeeze, shove, and cram until the van was packed as tight as the crowd in Times Square on New Year's Eve. Then I'd hold that last item with one hand and slam the hatch door with the other before anything could fall out. Who needs to see out the back window, anyway?

On one trip, we were several hours in and making good time. We had put a lot of miles behind us, and I stopped at the next roadside rest area. It was a nice place, too, with clean restrooms, picnic tables, and walking paths.

"Okay, team," let's hit the restrooms, meet back at the van, and hit the road again."

When I get back to the van, my son is digging through everything in the back.

He says, "Dad, where did you put my skateboard?"

"Why do you need that?" I ask.

He says, "Mom said we could stretch for a bit."

Well, naturally, I hadn't imagined he would need that till we got to Grandma's house.

My daughter gets back and asks where her scooter is—something else I didn't think we would need until we got there. It folded up nicely and tucked perfectly into a corner at the very bottom, behind the bags, along with my son's skateboard.

My wife wanders back and asks for the bag of condiments. I didn't even know there *was* a bag of condiments!

All right, people! We were stopping to pee—not stretch, exercise, and eat! (Dad getting hyper again. Dad overruled by Mom. Court adjourned.)

Ugh! I ended up unpacking almost everything! I was exasperated. This did not fit into the "quickly and efficiently" result I had in mind. My family wasn't too happy with my response, either.

That's what *working backward* does. It creates tunnel vision. It serves *you* and excludes others. It ignores impact. And it also causes you more pain in the long run.

Zombie Guy

It happens every day in business, too. And it causes frustration and confusion for employees.

Once, I was working with a group of managers, using mock scenarios to practice how we would address a problem with an employee. In one scenario, they had to talk with an employee who wasn't using the most current best practices at work.

The first person to volunteer says eagerly, "Oh, I want to be the employee!" That struck me as odd.

This guy opts to take the supporting role in the exercise, not the main role. That's like turning down the lead role in *The Walking Dead* to be one of a thousand zombies. But okay, why not? You can be the zombie.

The person playing the manager uses a direct approach: "You've been using outdated processes in your experiments. You need to keep up with the latest literature in the journals."

Zombie guy says, "Well, ordinarily I do. In fact, I've been spending hundreds of dollars every week on journals, doing exactly that. And in the last three meetings, you told us it was *critical* to cut expenses. So I did."

The manager says, "That's not what I meant." Zombie Guy says with a smirk, "Well, that's what you *said*."

Well played, Zombie, well played. Zombie Guy takes the lead role.

Zombie Guy goes on to say that this scenario actually happened to him. But in real life, he didn't get a chance to respond. His manager launched into a one-sided rant that attacked not only his abilities but his decision-making and his work ethic.

I asked him how it felt being talked to that way. He said, and I quote, "It was degrading."

Managing the result—cutting expenses—cost the manager in quality of work and in his relationship with the employee, and in the end, he lost a good employee. Zombie Guy quit.

> **WORKING BACKWARD...**
> MANAGING THE RESULT AND NOT YOUR ACTIONS.

Take a lesson from Zombie Guy. Learn to recognize when you're working backward, and become aware of the impact it's having.

Red Flags

There are three sure signs a person has bought into the Lie and is working backward: *dwelling, blaming, and making excuses*.

These are actionless, self-serving tactics that people use to defend themselves when something troublesome happens. I say "actionless" because none of these are actionable steps that move a situation forward or improve the outcome. They are reactions used to distance yourself from a situation that may reflect poorly on you.

Dwelling is talking or ruminating at length about a situation that is causing us problems. Usually, we're dwelling on it not to find a solution, but to work out a scenario in which we're not responsible. And that is backward indeed!

Blaming is an attempt to shift responsibility for something that went wrong. From the moment we start thinking, *it's not me; it's them,* we are working backward.

Excuses are reasons or explanations for failure that point somewhere other than yourself. Definitely backward.

When you use these tactics, the very thing you are trying to protect—your reputation, image, or ego— takes a big hit.

For instance, if you are struggling to meet objectives and you think, *I have incompetent employees,* you're working backward, still managing the result instead of your actions.

You wanted good results and got bad results instead. Now you want to shift responsibility for the poor results to the actions of your employees. (And yes, your employees are responsible for their results, but that is a different conversation. Right now, the magnifying glass is on you.)

The focus is all wrong. You have disconnected your actions from the results. If you truly have incompetent employees, it's because of what you have or haven't done. And yes, you read that right. The choice *not* to do something has consequences. Therefore, inaction is also an action. Not to decide is to decide.

As a manager, you are responsible for hiring competent employees. You are also responsible for *developing* competent employees. By focusing on the result, you are leaving yourself out of the equation, as if actions didn't matter.

Dwelling, blaming, and making excuses will never change the outcome. But it will destroy your credibility with those you follow and those you lead.

Nowhere to Run

Behaving as if results were the only thing that matters creates a trap that sets you up for failure. I know; I've ensnared myself in that trap.

The problem was, I didn't even know I was *in* the trap, until something went wrong. That's when I would panic. *It's embarrassing,* I would think. *This is painful. I can't stay here. I've got to get out.* I was willing to chew off a leg to get out of that trap. Here's my escape plan.

When something went wrong, I would do an immediate assessment: *Was that us, or was it them?* (In other words, looking for someone to blame.)

Then I'd rehash the issue over and over, either in my head or with someone else. Sometimes both. Sometimes in my head while I was with someone else.

So as I was assessing (i.e., dwelling), I would make all the assumptions I could about all the things I was uncertain about, so that I could blame other people and events. Basically, anyone or anything that wasn't me was fair game. That way, if I was asked anything about the situation, I had a perfectly good, well-reasoned response (excuse).

No matter what logic or metric we use, the Lie convinces us to forget all reason. It steers us away from leadership mode and drives us into self-preservation mode. And it feels as though the only way to preserve yourself

BLAMING SOMEONE FOR NOT GETTING WHAT YOU WANT WON'T GET YOU WHAT YOU WANT.

is to use the tactics of the Lie.

No one is immune to this. Because when something happens that's not supposed to happen, the Lie will be sitting right on your shoulder and whispering in your ear, telling you about everything that is at risk. Your reputation. Your image. Your credibility.

Once the Lie has you in its grip, it doesn't let you act. Instead, it gets you to *re*act. You start giving your employees orders to manage the result. You issue reprimands: *"You need to cut expenses." "You need to manage your time better." "You need to speak up in meetings." "You need to be a team player.*

Don't be misled. The Lie is a liar and trickster. It will get you to focus on the wrong thing every time.

Vicious Cycle

When you believe the Lie, you end up working backward. That's because, when the result becomes more important than your actions, the actions you do take become misaligned. Ultimately, they become counterproductive to the intended result. Your actions become self-serving when they should be serving other stakeholders. And having a *neutral* effect on others is never enough—your actions must *improve* outlook, enthusiasm, and performance for everyone in your orbit: the team, the customer, the business, the community. Even the custodian, the maintenance staff, and the security guard should be benefiting from your actions. Anytime you ignore or dismiss others in favor of the result you seek, you end up with problems.

In 2015, Vice Admiral Joseph Aucoin was selected to lead the Seventh Fleet. At the time, China was expanding into disputed waters, and North Korea was testing ballistic missiles. The admiral was receiving orders from the Pentagon to carry out more and more missions.

The admiral was reluctant. He found that the fleet was understaffed, poorly trained, and worked to exhaustion. He repeatedly warned his superiors of the situation. They disregarded his warnings and told him to calm down and get the job done. That is a "results are the only thing that matters" instruction.

Sure enough, on June 17, 2017, the USS *Fitzgerald,* a navy destroyer, collided with a giant cargo ship off the coast of Japan, ripping a huge hole in the destroyer's hull. Seven sailors drowned in their sleeping quarters. It was the deadliest naval disaster in four decades.

Two months later, another accident occurred. The USS *John S. McCain* turned directly in front of a thirty-thousand-ton oil tanker. Ten more sailors died.

After these events, the Naval Surface Group was formed to oversee maintenance, training, and certification. Ships and crews now receive dedicated training and maintenance time. If the NSG determines that a particular ship is not ready for a mission, it will remain in port until it is.

So, what mission are you focused on? Is the result more important than your actions? Are you dismissing the input of others to attain it? Will it take two separate disasters before you act? Here's the kicker: **A problem is also a result.** It is the result of your misaligned actions.

And if, at this point, you continue to work backward, the "problem" is the new result, which you then try to manage. This leads to more misaligned actions, which lead to more problems. For instance, say a manager running a production group needs to produce fifty thousand units to fulfill the promise a sales rep made to a customer. To create a sense of urgency, he tells the employees, "You have to meet this deadline no matter what it takes. If you don't, we're going to be in trouble."

The lead on the production line says, "We're already at full production capacity."

To which the manager replies, "If you can't do it, I'll get someone who can."

In the effort to meet the demand, the production lead directs the team to skip the quality-assurance process to save time.

Result: The company meets the deadline, but the customer complains about the quality and returns 20 percent of the units.

Problem (new result): Quality issues.

Manager: "This is not acceptable. I don't want to see quality issues anymore. Stick to the SOPs" (standard operating procedures).

Lead: Directs employees to strictly adhere to the SOPs

Employees: Comply with all SOPs.

Result: Quality goes up. Output goes down.

Problem (new result): Difficulty fulfilling the next large order.

It's a vicious cycle that takes you further and further away from what you want.

Breaking the Cycle

If you want to build a business or career, make money, be a better leader or parent, strengthen a relationship, discover a cure, win a championship, or get healthy, you must become **actively aware** of when you are working backward.

Active awareness starts with acknowledgment. You must acknowledge when the result has become more important than your actions.

When a result is more important than *anything* else, you will soon find yourself sacrificing *everything* else. You will sacrifice principles, trust, relationships, even ethics. So you must ask yourself, *Am I willing to make these kinds of sacrifices for the result I want?*

> *The way we choose to get to where we're going defines what it's going to be like when we get there.*
>
> -Seth Godin

When a result is more important than anything else, we *react*. We become defensive or dismissive. We shift responsibility.

When a result is more important than anything else, you will experience problems. Problems are where you are most susceptible to working backward. If you don't acknowledge this, you will perpetuate the vicious cycle.

So, what's the number one problem you're wrestling with right now? What issue has its grip on you?

- Are your employees hard at work on the wrong priorities?
- Do employees bring up potential problems, or do you get blindsided when the problem manifests?
- Are competing goals putting a strain on limited resources?
- When you pose questions to your team, do they chime in with useful ideas, or do you hear only the chirring of crickets?
- Do your meetings lack engagement? Are there backroom meetings after those meetings?
- Is poor communication between functional groups slowing progress?
- Are sales up yet profits are down?
- Are department-head conflicts playing out in front of the teams?
- Is quality going downhill while customer complaints are on the rise?

Now, active awareness alone will not get you what you want. It won't change your situation. It merely lays the groundwork so you can refocus your efforts on the things that actually matter. Don't get me wrong. Active awareness is absolutely crucial. But it's only the first step in the process. The next chapter, "Identifying Actions," is every bit as vital to the process, because *how you decide* to get what you want shapes the environment where you live and work.

Questions That Matter...

- What mission are you focused on?
- What actions are you putting off?
- What price will you pay if you don't act?

Chapter Seven

IDENTIFYING ACTIONS

Every action is like a boomerang. You put something out; you always get something back. So if you take random actions, it's going to lead to random results. You must identify the actions that lead to what is *supposed* to happen.

The first time I threw an actual boomerang, it was a heavy wooden one. I went in front of my house and threw it down the street as hard as I could. I thought it was *supposed* to come back. Instead, it shot away like a rocket toward the horizon. Not a bad start. Then, all of a sudden, it pitched downward, bounced off the ground, and ricocheted off my neighbor's house. *Hmmm. Maybe it's defective or broken* (blaming).

So I tested that theory. I ran over, picked it up, turned around, and threw it back down the street the other way. Again it shot straight out toward the horizon. This time, it started to rise and turn. *Yes! That's what a boomerang is supposed to do.* Then my neighbor's window got in the way (making excuses). Ugh …

At the Bottom of the Box

It was getting to be an expensive practice session, so I decided to take it inside. No, I didn't throw the wooden one again. I had ordered a box full of different types. I grabbed a small foam one from the box. I threw it. It shot off to the right and hit a lamp. No damage this time. I grabbed another, threw it. It shot off to the left and hit the ceiling. *Well, this is discouraging.*

And as I reached into the box for another one, I saw a white booklet at the bottom. I pulled it out. The cover was imprinted with bold block letters: INSTRUCTIONS. *I wish I had seen that before the window incident.*

As I looked through the instruction booklet, nothing in it told me to focus on the boomerang coming back, although that is what it is supposed to do.

It didn't tell me to persuade, intimidate, or coax it into coming back. It didn't tell me to "do whatever it takes." It didn't say any of that.

- But it did tell me how to *prepare* the boomerang so it was capable of coming back.
- It gave me *techniques* on how to hold it and throw it so it would come back.
- It even gave me *tips* on how to throw it in harmony with the elements of the environment. So if the wind was blowing, it would still come back.

It told me all the things to do up until the point I actually released the boomerang, so that what was supposed to happen actually did happen.

The Big Question

If you want what's supposed to happen to actually happen, you don't manage the result. You manage your actions—the part that comes *before* the result. The part of the universal law that you actually control.

The question is always **How do I *cause* the effect that I want?**

When you realize your team is not meeting its sales goals, telling them in a state of panic, "You need to sell more!" does nothing to generate more sales. You're trying to manage the result. If you want to improve sales, what causes better sales? What actions can you take to improve sales? Are you hiring qualified people? What actions does it take to make good salespeople better? Is your training focused on the right actions? Do your actions support those actions, or merely push for the result? What part do you actually control in delivering the intended result?

When you learn that your child is failing in school, telling them in a state of panic, "You need to pick up your grades!" does nothing to improve grades. You're trying to manage the result. Are you acting or *re*acting? What actions support the child to succeed in school? What's getting in the way of the result you want? Does it have to do with structure? Does it have to do with study habits? Does it have to do with the child's learning approach? What part do you control in delivering the intended result?

I want to be clear. I'm not telling you to micromanage the actions of others. I'm saying to micromanage YOUR actions. Pay attention to what you're doing, and consider the impact on those around you.

If you are facing a problem, what actions should you be managing?

If you are thinking, *I can't trust my employees,* consider the actions you took before the current result (distrust) began. You either hired or inherited them. Either way, you are responsible. Therefore, you must take all actions necessary to move that team from where they are right now to where you expect them to be. So what actions will begin to develop that trust?

If a manager tells an employee, "You need to manage your time better," it isn't all that helpful. It can be confusing and frustrating to an employee, because it's a directive to manage the result. Somehow, the manager sees that the employee is not performing to a particular standard. If the employee managed her time better, she would deliver on that expectation.

Let me take the employee's perspective. I'm doing everything I can in the best way that I know how, to get done what you're asking me to do. I keep getting more work piled on top of my already full plate. If I knew how to manage my time in a way that reduces the pressure and stress I'm feeling, I would do it. So when you say to manage my time better, what does that really mean? How am I not managing my time? Are you saying I need to spend more time at work? Is the pace not quick enough? Is my focus not what you would like? What are the things you want me to focus on? Do you think I should manage my time more like you? What would you change about my approach? How am I falling short of your expectations? What things am I doing that you feel I should drop? What are your priorities? Should I reduce the *quality* of the work so the *quantity* of work rises?

Most employees don't just show up for work and intentionally do things to make themselves look bad and undermine their manager. The same goes for managers. Most managers don't act deliberately to disengage employees, make them miserable, and torpedo their results. But random actions can sure make it feel that way.

What Is Supposed to Happen

Identifying actions is an intentional process to pinpoint what you control, so that you can provide useful support to deal effectively with the situation at hand.

Taking a page from the boomerang instruction booklet, consider actions around preparation, techniques, and tips so that what's supposed to happen actually happens. Ask:

- What do *I* need to do to *help* people *prepare* themselves so they are *capable* of delivering what is expected?
  - Do they know what's expected?
  - Have I expressed the expectations directly and clearly?
  - Do they have the authority to make the decisions necessary to carry out the objective?
  - Do they have the necessary resources?
  - What skills do they need in order to achieve the expectation?

- What *techniques* could I use that would *support* them in returning what's expected?
  - Do they require training?
  - Could I coach them to meet the expectation?
  - Would a mentor help?
  - Do I even understand the employee's challenge?
  - Do I need to engage the employee? Ask questions? Share information? Listen?

- What **tips** could I share that give the team or team member an advantage in delivering what is expected, despite the challenges?
  - What guidance can I offer about the task, the project, or the key players?
  - What insights can I share about the culture, the company, the customer, the client, or the industry?

Actions, not reactions, create the result you want. Ask the questions. Answer the questions. Then follow the instructions. If you don't, you're bound to break a window.

Shortcuts

In management, we break a lot of windows unnecessarily. It usually happens when we take shortcuts. I'm not talking about a better or more efficient way to do something. I'm talking about going the easy route to avoid the pain or discomfort of doing the hard part—the part we know we should be doing.

Years ago, I delivered a week-long conference with another speaker. My colleague, Allen, whom I had just met for the first time, told the audience that his doctor told him if he didn't eat less and exercise more, he wouldn't see his children grow up. So he lost 135 pounds. I was impressed, and the audience was touched. They would give him a round of applause.

When Allen and I got together for dinner in the evenings, he wasn't choosing a healthy diet. Months later, I worked with him again. He had gained back more than half the weight. In the evening, we had dinner together again. I asked what happened.

Allen revealed to me that before we met, he had his stomach stapled to lose weight. He went on to say he hadn't been following the doctor's instructions. He never changed his eating habits and he hadn't been exercising. The gastric bypass surgery was for him just a shortcut to avoid the harder work of changing his diet and doing regular exercise.

The thing is, a shortcut can never substitute for the real work that must be done. Without the proper actions, success will be fleeting at best.

Who hasn't looked in the mirror and said, "I need to get in shape"?

It's what we do *next* that makes all the difference. The temptation, of course, is to search for the latest fad or magic pill that will transform us without our ever breaking a sweat or skipping dessert.

You want to lose weight or get in shape? You know what to do to make that happen. Weight and fitness are reactions. They're reactions to *what* you eat, *how much* you eat, and how much you *exercise*. It's that basic. But somehow, we want to believe we can get the result without the sacrifice. This happens to all of us in various ways.

"I can fix that."

I tend to think I can fix anything and save the money of having someone else do it. So when something in my home needs fixing, I don't think, *hire a professional.* I think, *Oh, I can fix that.*

When I was living in Georgia, I was out mowing the lawn. It was hot and humid. I was in loose shorts and a T-shirt. I was dripping with sweat, and dirt and grass clippings were sticking to me all over. Then I ran over a nest of yellow jackets. Did you know they sometimes burrow in the ground? I sure didn't. I got stung a few times and ran inside to get away, slinging off my T-shirt and swatting as I ran. I slung around a few four-letter words. My wife said, "Call pest control."

And spend the money when I can do it just as well myself? I've got this.

Sitting on the sidewalk was a can of gas for the mower. I poured some of it down the hole. Okay, I poured a lot. And I

> **SHORTCUT...**
> AN ATTEMPT TO AVOID THE PAIN OF DOING THE HARD WORK THAT LEADS TO BETTER RESULTS.

even decided to light it. Surely that added touch would ensure there were no escapees. I stumbled backward as a ball of flame rolled through the air. At that moment, I wished I had watched a bit more of the Discovery Channel.

Apparently, yellow jackets are like rabbits or prairie dogs in that their burrows have multiple exits! And it looks as though they do more fire drills than most of us, because they were fast. As I'm standing there staring at the hole, I get stung a few more times. I start running toward the house again. This time, they're chasing me! My arms are flailing as I get stung several more times. *Pop*—arm. *Pop*—neck. *Pop*—face. *Pop*—back. *Pop, pop*—both calves. *Pop*—thigh.

I ran through the house, up the stairs, and straight into the shower. As I'm standing in the shower with my clothes on, *pop*—on my thigh, under my shorts! And *pop*—on my back, under my shirt!

In the end, I paid two professionals for that shortcut: the pest-control company and a doctor. Oh, and the doctor looked me up and down, and she said, "Okay, Jim, I get all the stings, but how'd you end up with singed eyebrows?" (Long, embarrassed sigh.)

With shortcuts, there is always an unanticipated cost.

Car-tastrophe

Years ago, Volkswagen took a shortcut. It had a goal to be the biggest seller of cars in the world. The thing getting in the way of reaching that goal was that its diesel models couldn't pass the US emissions tests. So Volkswagen's engineers designed what they called a "dual-strategy software." That sounds much nicer than "fraudulent shortcut," doesn't it?

The software would detect when the engine was undergoing emissions testing. When the car was connected to the machine, it would turn on all the emission controls so it could pass the test. When the software detected that the car was disconnected from the emissions-testing equipment, it would cut off all the emission controls. So in real-world driving, the cars ended up emitting up to forty times the legal limit of nitrogen oxides. Those are pollutants that cause asthma and other health problems.

At the end of 2017, that shortcut had cost the company $30 billion.

Less turns out much less

A shortcut has the allure of costing "less" effort, time, and money. When the result is the only thing that matters, there will be less deliberation, less thought, less effort, less pain, less stress, less confrontation, less awkwardness, less exposure, less truthfulness, less responsibility, or less time spent.

Shortcuts will ensure that your success, if you have any at all, is short-lived. You will sacrifice something.

For example, let's suppose you have a team member who is struggling to deliver what is expected. In an attempt to get the team member to improve, you point to a star performer on the team and say, "You need to be more like her." It takes far less effort and time to compare the two employees and leave it up to the one who's falling short to figure out what he needs to do differently than it does to contemplate what actions *you* can take to support the individual in his skill development.

It takes less effort and less work to meet the sales target by lowering the price of a product than it does to think about what you can do to improve your sales strategy in the long run.

It's less stressful and less awkward to give hints to an employee about what you want them to change than it does to have an honest, up-front conversation about what needs to change.

It's less awkward to vent to coworkers, family, or friends than it is to talk directly and respectfully to the person you have an issue with.

It's easier and there's less pushback if you do the task yourself rather than work with the individual so she can perform on her own. And what works for employees is just as true for children.

It's less time consuming to pick up fast food than to prepare a meal as part of a healthy lifestyle. If *we* don't focus on the right things, neither will our children.

It's far less stressful to clean up after your children than it is to teach them to care for themselves, their belongings, and the people around them.

The odd thing is that when we do less, we're surprised when we don't get more.

Cheating

Want your kid to get accepted into one of the top universities in the country even though he hasn't done the work to earn the admission?

That's exactly what happened in 2019. Federal prosecutors indicted dozens of wealthy parents, college test administrators, and athletic coaches in a bribery-and-fraud scheme. The investigation found that these wealthy parents paid up to $1.2 million to have their children accepted into some of the most elite colleges in the United States, such as USC, Yale, and Stanford.

The investigation, nicknamed Operation Varsity Blues, found two criminal schemes: cheating on standardized tests, and college acceptance bribery. The prosecutors said, and the courts agreed, that the parents paid a college test-prep organization to help the students cheat. They would either have a surrogate take the test for the student or have the test proctor correct the answers. College coaches were also bribed to designate applicants as athletic recruits even though they knew nothing about the sports that they supposedly played.

Who was hurt? All the students who put years of effort into developing their knowledge base or honing their athletic abilities. They were denied an opportunity, not by peer competition but by cheating adults. Also hurt were the students who were the supposed beneficiaries of the fraud. Their parents were setting a terrible example for them while also eloquently delivering their unspoken conviction that their child didn't have what it takes to succeed!

Getting more by doing less?

Shortcuts are an attempt to get more by doing less. And you can't get more from people by doing less.

- You can't build trust by trusting less.
- You can't earn respect by showing less respect.
- You can't resolve communication problems by communicating less.
- You can't develop competent employees by training less.
- You can't correct a performance issue by giving an employee less to do.

There are no shortcuts to building relationships, trust, respect, credibility, or integrity. Shortcuts can never replace the work that must be done for long-term success.

To make sure you are focusing on the things that matter, identify the appropriate actions. Ask the questions first, follow through on the needed actions, and NO SHORTCUTS.

Questions That Matter...

- *What actions occurring in* your *workplace are taking away opportunities for deserving people?*

- *How are you trying to get more by doing less?*

- *Where are you taking shortcuts in your work and life?*

- *What actions do you need to take to ensure that others are taking appropriate actions?*

Chapter Eight

ASSESSING AND ADJUSTING

The term *assessing* implies that we have a measuring stick to gauge our success. And we do. It's called the "result." So if we get the result we want, we're successful.

The problem is that the result only measures where you are at a given point in time. It's the *outcome* of your actions. But it says nothing about the *quality* of those actions.

Team Member Overboard!

To illustrate this point, suppose I'm leading a ten-person team in a big wooden rowboat in the middle of the ocean. Yeah, I know, it sounds like the world's worst team-building exercise. But just roll with me here—all will become clear.

Along the way, I notice the boat is sinking. I mean, it's supposed to float, right? Immediately, I grab three people and pitch them overboard. The boat rises. That's what I wanted, so it's all good. I see this as a success.

But the three treading water with no life jackets probably don't see it that way. They are a bit confused. They don't know *why* they are in the water or *what* they did that got them there. Nonetheless, we leave them behind, and the rest of us row away.

As we pull away from our bewildered swimmers, it is more difficult now, because we are down three rowers. At first, the seven still aboard are mostly just glad they are not the ones in the water. But like the ones in the water, they, too, are confused. They have no idea *why* the boat was sinking, or *what* they did or didn't do that kept them in the boat. But they row a bit harder anyway. Why? Well, when facing the possibility of being thrown in the water, do what you know: ROW!

All the while, their "sense of security" flares are firing off like the Fourth of July. A few decide to put on a life jacket. They scan Monster.com. Peruse Indeed's website. Search LinkedIn. Next thing I know, two of the seven remaining rowers tell me they're leaving for a land job, and my boat starts to sink again.

Collateral Damage

When *results are the only thing that matters,* you will throw people overboard—or maybe just under the bus. Either way, it's an attempt to get what you want at the expense of those around you. That's called *collateral damage.*

Results don't account for collateral damage. That's why they are a faulty measure of success. A leader's intent should be to uplift and guide others to success, not to climb over them or use them for their own personal ends. You are capable of both achieving the result AND treating people respectfully and professionally.

By definition, collateral damage is not deliberate. But if you ever hope to minimize it, you must become aware of the possibility that it may occur. If you don't make it your business to assess the possible collateral damage, the fallout could be costly to people, the organization, and you.

So what's *your* measuring stick?

Whether you're rowing a boat, building a business, forming a team, or forging a relationship, success hinges directly on the *quality of the actions you take.*

It's why you need a measuring stick other than a result to **assess your actions.** The stick should measure the things that DO matter: people, relationships, culture, standards, expectations, and integrity. The measuring stick you will use is rooted in your values. Ask yourself, are my intended actions …

- professional?

- respectful?

- truthful?

- fair?

- inclusive?

- supportive?

- consistent?

- beneficial?

- the right thing to do?

This measuring stick will keep you taking deliberate actions that move you forward with integrity and consistency.

ATM

I watched this play out one time as I was checking into a hotel in Orlando. It was a huge resort and conference center. The lobby was packed. It was like a bar at happy hour. Loud. Lots of partying. Drinking. Laughter. There was even a long line to get in.

As I stood in line, above all the people noise there was a constant beeping sound.

After a couple of minutes, the woman in front of me turns to me and says, "What's that noise?"

I look over, and near the check-in counter is a bank machine with money sticking out of the slot. I say, "Looks as if someone forgot their money. The machine should have pulled it back in by now."

The woman walks over to the machine, takes the money from the slot, and steps over to the check-in counter. Handing the cash to one of the clerks behind the counter, she says with a smile, "Somebody left their money in the machine. I'm sure they'll come looking for it. If not, the bank will."

Watching from the outside, it was easy to see that the lady's actions were informed by some sort of ethical code. Call it *integrity* or *honesty* or *doing what is right*. But that's not the end of the story.

When she steps back in line, the guy in front of her turns to her and says, "Why didn't you keep that? They're just going to keep it anyway."

As you can tell from the example, a result is not an ethical guide. Although this was merely a comment the guy made, the point at which we are willing to sacrifice our values, integrity, or sense of decency is precisely the point where we have lost our way. And it happens because we have let the result become the measure of our success.

TWYST

These two people saw things very differently. Their perspectives will lead them to very different outcomes that affect others in very different ways. This brings us to my next point.

You must be aware of your T.W.Y.S.T. It stands for **The Way You See Things**. (I'll use *TWYST* as a noun going forward.) Your TWYST leads to a possible course of action, which you are then able to assess.

By *adjusting* your TWYST, you can open up different courses of action. This is important because it is part of a process that determines not only where you end up but also what the culture will be like when you get there. And it happens very quickly. Here's how it works:

Every result starts with your TWYST. It is the way you perceive a situation, job, or person.

From your TWYST, you generate an *attitude.* By definition, your attitude is an emotion or mental position toward what you see. Now, people love to say attitude is everything. And I agree to a point. It is important. But you don't just wake up with the attitude of, say, "I'm angry" for no reason. Your attitude emanates from your TWYST.

Your attitude directs your level of *responsibility toward your obligations.* Your level of responsibility toward those obligations could be high or low. If it is low, you focus strictly on what's good for you. It's a self-preservation mode. If it's high, you look to benefit not only yourself but also those around you. It is the mode of a true leader.

To improve your effectiveness within any culture, you have to shift the responsibility for your obligations from low to high, because this determines the *actions* you take.

The actions you take, in turn, deliver certain *results*. And the cycle continues from there.

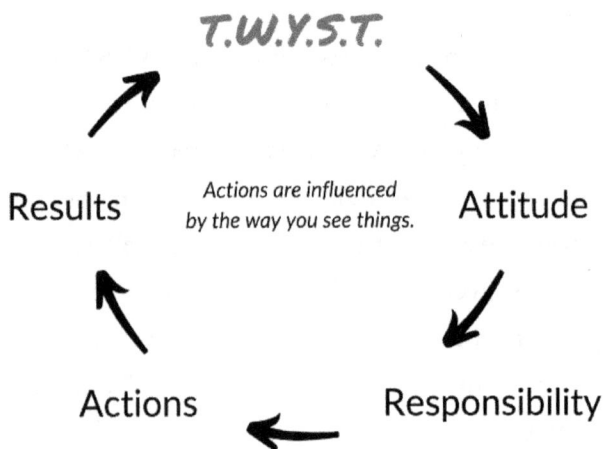

T.W.Y.S.T.

Results   Actions are influenced   Attitude
by the way you see things.

Actions   Responsibility

And once again, it's why results aren't what matters. It's your *actions* that matter. And adjusting your TWYST can improve the quality of your actions.

Shifting the Workload

Here's an example of where your TWYST leads to the result you want, but your actions negatively affect people and the culture.

Let's suppose you are responsible for the completion of a project, and you have a poorly performing employee on your team. He is not meeting expectations, and this is putting you behind schedule. You see the employee as incompetent and apathetic (TWYST). You become frustrated (attitude). You immediately get concerned that your manager will see you in a bad light for the deficiency on this project, which shifts your focus to *you* (low level of responsibility). To get on track and not look bad in your manager's eyes, you shift work from the poorly performing team member to a peak-performing team member (action). The project gets completed (result).

That's what's supposed to happen, right? Well, yes, you solved the problem and you delivered, so your manager should view you positively. Thus, it worked out—for the moment.

The concern here is that your TWYST has led to a shortcut—the act of shifting work from the *poor* performer to the *peak* performer. You see this as a quicker route to the result, because that's your true focus. Whatever the reason, you may recall, there is always an associated cost in taking a shortcut. Allow me to carry the scenario out further so you can see the cost of that decision.

This one shortcut leads to multiple reactions. One is that the poor performer, who is not meeting expectations, is required to do less work and won't know what to do differently. Thus, he remains in an underproductive state. Another reaction is that the *peak* performer, who is already going above and beyond expectations, is required to do more work!

If you maintain this TWYST and continue to resolve performance issues by shifting work this way, the peak performer eventually gets overloaded, burns out, and quits. Then you are left shorthanded with the underdeveloped team member. Stress goes up, morale goes down, and results get worse.

In the long run, the dynamic is not good for anyone, including you. So let's look at this differently.

Flipping your TWYST

It's the same scenario, but let's adjust your TWYST.

Once again, you are responsible for the completion of a project. You have a poorly performing employee on your team. This time, you see the employee as the capable, high-potential person you hired, who happens to be struggling with a particular issue, and your role is to develop her abilities and bring out her potential (TWYST). You immediately adopt a supportive approach (attitude). You see how guidance can help her develop security in her position by increasing the value of her contribution to the team. This shifts your focus to what's good for the employee, the team, and the organization (high level of responsibility). To meet this responsibility, you have a one-to-one meeting, determine what is needed, and coach the employee (action). The work gets done (result).

That's what's supposed to happen, right? Yes indeed, but this time, your TWYST has led to actions that have numerous benefits.

Along with getting the work done, you now have a more skilled employee who will perform better on projects going forward. You have a better working relationship with the employee, and the other team members have a competent colleague who adds value so others—including you—don't have to take on extra burdens. This improves morale and the functioning of the whole group, which is a benefit to the organization or company. Moreover, your credibility with both your team and your manager gets a boost as well.

The question is not what you look at, but what you see.

-Henry David Thoreau

Marcus flips his TWYST

When I met Marcus in one of my seminars, he had just been promoted to regional manager for a paint store chain. He went from managing one store to twelve. It was a big role, and he was excited about the opportunity, even more so for the boost it provided in supporting his family.

He told me he was having trouble with one of his store managers, Lucas. Although Lucas had been a manager for years, his store's performance was mediocre at best, and it began drifting downward. Marcus could see that Lucas's management style was affecting the employees, sales, and customer feedback, and not in a good way. Marcus assured me that he had given Lucas every chance to turn his performance around: support, guidance, training, and resetting expectations. Nothing changed, and Lucas didn't seem to care, either. Here is a condensed version of the rest of the conversation:

Marcus: Where do I go from here?

Me: Have you considered replacing him?

Marcus: It's complicated. The guy is good friends with the owner. I feel as if my hands are tied. If I fire him, the owner might get mad at me. And he could hire Lucas back; then my credibility would be shot.

Me: Let's look at this situation in a different way. When the owner needed a regional manager, he promoted you, not his friend. That decision tells me that he trusts your abilities, your decision-making, and your commitment. It also tells me that he bases his actions on what is best for the business and its employees. Why aren't you basing your actions on the same thing?

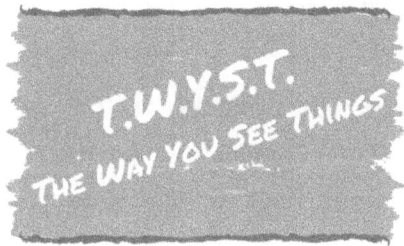

Your credibility lives or dies by what you do and what you don't do. The situation right now is that you have a store that is losing money, and a manager who shows little interest in improving the situation.

If you leave this situation as is, are your actions supporting what you were hired to do, or are they influenced by some notion you have about the manager's relationship with the owner? Is it good for the business and the employees to leave an unmotivated and inattentive manager in this leadership role? Do you think it's good leadership if a store's doors are locked when the employees arrive for work?

Marcus took the time to think about his TWYST. The next day, he decided to do what was best for everyone and released Lucas. Marcus notified the owner via email so he would be aware of the situation.

Marcus told me he received an email from the owner that said, "It's about time."

Wearing Blinders

In New Orleans, you can get a tour of the French Quarter by horse and carriage. The guides give a colorful commentary on the history of the city while maneuvering in and out of the vehicular traffic and crowds of people. Cars are loud and honking. People want to pet the horses. To minimize distractions, the horses wear blinders. This way, they can focus only on what's in front of them, without getting spooked by sudden movements on either side.

Taking action without first assessing and adjusting is like putting on blinders. They narrow your field of vision so that you see only what's in front of you. So it's easier to focus—because you can't see what's going on around you. So you miss how those around you are being affected.

Assessing and adjusting enable you to consider the impact of your actions so you're not working blindly.

Taking Off the Blinders

I once got some coaching from Larry Winget. A professional speaker and six-time *Wall Street Journal* and *New York Times* bestselling author, Larry is an insightful writer, and he's tremendous onstage.

Each of us in a small group was looking to improve our craft as a speaker. Everyone was firing off questions. Each question essentially asked, *"What do I need to do to become a better speaker?"* Our concerns ranged from delivery style to stage presence, to body language, to storytelling. Larry responded in detail to every question, and we all eagerly wrote down the tips.

Then he said, "You can do everything I said and still not be good."

—Whoa, wait a minute … What?

And it's his next statement that has resonated and stuck with me ever since. He said, "If you think like a speaker, you'll never be a great speaker. Only when you learn to think like the audience do you have a chance of being a great speaker."

Not one of us was looking at improving our game from that perspective. No one asked a question from that vantage point. All our questions focused on our techniques. Techniques without understanding are doomed to be ineffective. And so a blinder was removed.

We all understand that when we speak, we have an audience. This is true whether the audience is a dozen people we manage, or a single team member. The question is still the same: Are you serving them from the best perspective?

So Larry's advice is sound for becoming a better manager as well. Just modify the terminology: *If you think like a manager, you'll never be a great manager. Only when you learn to think like those you lead do you have a chance of being a great manager.*

The Way Forward

Every day, you must strive to see what others see. Strive to understand their pain, recognize their struggles, and anticipate their challenges. This way, you can better identify the actions that will support and guide those you serve, while minimizing the negative residual effects that can have a long-term impact.

Through assessing and adjusting, you can tailor your actions to foster a healthy environment for everyone—an environment that promotes trust, credibility, and reliability. Make it part of your daily practice, and you will see your values, standards, and expectations upheld, thus protecting what is important to you as well. As this becomes a habit, you will see an improvement in the quality of your actions, the quality of your outcomes, and the quality of your relationships.

Questions That Matter...

- Is my perspective holding me back from doing what is best?

- Are my actions respectful of those involved?

- Will this action support and add value to the employee and the organization?

- How does this approach support the work culture?

- Will I be putting someone at a disadvantage so that I gain the advantage?

- Would I still support this action if I were on the receiving end?

- Is this the same action I would take if my child were on the receiving end?

- Is this action honest, direct, and kind?

- Is it ethical?

- How will this advance the business?

- In what way could this action undermine the team?

- How could this action hurt our image and reputation?

Chapter Nine

IMPACT

I talked about impact in the first chapter, "Gary the Chef." I said, *You may not always see that you're doing it. You may not always recognize how you're doing it. You may not even know when you're doing it. But you* ARE *doing it.*

Everyone Leads, Everyone Manages

Although the focal point of this book has been the leadership of people in the workplace, we all affect people daily. Whether you serve in the role of a business owner, spouse, partner, entrepreneur, friend, family member, parent, colleague, employee, instructor, coach, patient, neighbor, student, or mentor, in each role, you seek something. As a business owner, you may focus on opening a certain number of new branches over the next three years. As a spouse, you may desire a more meaningful relationship. As a coach, you may focus on developing a superstar or a team. As a parent, your prime objective may be to raise a happy, capable child. As a student, it may be a degree you're after.

Whatever result you seek, you will find yourself steering a course through your and other people's problems, aspirations, and relationships. Make no mistake: navigating any of these requires *everyone* to lead and manage. There are seemingly infinite definitions of "leadership" and "management." I'm not here to debate the fine nuances. For our purposes, these two terms are inextricable.

Whether you find yourself helping a fellow team member develop a new skill, helping your child with an ethical dilemma, or guiding your friend through a rough patch, to succeed professionally and personally you must master both leading and managing.

Taking the Lead

When you choose to lead, your actions have a broader impact than if you were flying solo. And so will your *lack* of action, because it allows other actions to prevail. For instance ...

- If blaming is a common practice and no one calls it out, blaming will be the prevailing action. The culture will degrade into defensiveness, with every team member for her- or himself. Every time something goes wrong, more time and energy will be spent on infighting to deflect responsibility than on resolving the issues. Or ...

- If yelling is a tactic used for disagreements and no one calls it out, yelling becomes the prevailing action. The culture will degrade into intimidation and humiliation. And you shouldn't be surprised when people sit on problems and are reluctant to participate in meetings.

You must step up to the inherent responsibilities that come with the role of managing and leading people. Everyone deserves to work in a culture where they have an opportunity to apply their talents, grow from their experience, and thrive. To get that opportunity, they need a manager who knows how to redirect their focus onto the things that matter.

This comes from the three components we have been discussing:

1. **Be actively aware** of when you are working backward, and do not fight universal laws. You cannot circumvent reality to get what you want. Remember, "results are what matters" is a contagion that has led to a pandemic of mismanagement. Actions lead to results, and not the other way around. Be aware of your focus.

2. **Identify the actions** that "cause" the outcomes you want. Ask the appropriate questions. I have no doubt that you know the answers, or know where to find them, to resolve issues. And yes, I know that it takes more effort or more risk than you had hoped for. Don't let that seduce you into using a shortcut. Follow the instructions.

3. **Assess** your actions, using your values as a measuring stick. Remember, the perspective you hold influences your actions, so **adjust** your perspective to reflect those values. It's the *quality* of your actions that determines your success.

Forming New Habits

The Lie is a bad narrative that gets repeated over and over. Then we replay it over and over in our head. Then we put it into practice over and over. And there's truth in the old cliché "practice makes perfect." So if you practice these bad practices diligently, in the end you're just going to be really good at doing the wrong things!

Bad habits make things easier. It's easier to focus on results and ignore the collateral damage. It's easier to shrug your shoulders and say, "At least I got the result," and become the hero of your own story. It's easier to maintain the bad narrative and blame others when things don't go as intended—much, much easier.

Easier, yes, but does it make things better? Does it make you better? Does it make your people better? Does it make the business better? Does it make your perspective better? Does it make your actions and the actions of others better? Does it create a better impact? Of course not! It's time to separate yourself from the bad narrative and the bad habits it perpetuates.

BAD HABITS...
MAKE THINGS EASIER FOR YOU BUT WORSE FOR OTHERS.
GOOD HABITS...
MAKE THINGS BETTER FOR EVERYONE.

Bad habits make things easier. Good habits make things better. To become the kind of manager people want to work for, you need to replace the old *results matter* narrative with the new *actions matter* narrative. Then practice the three components, *raising your awareness, identifying actions, and assessing and adjusting,* daily until they become your natural way of thinking and working. It is better for the culture, better for the people, and better for the business. And that's what makes it better for you.

Chapter Ten

THE REVERSAL

And there you have it: the path to reverse the mismanagement pandemic. A path that puts people first. A path that balances the needs of those people with the needs of the business. A path that supports the responsibilities of your role while building your credibility, reputation, and integrity for the long term.

The question I have for you is, *Are you willing to follow this path?*

It will not be easy. Others will test you. Not out of any bad intent, but because they do not see how the Lie that *results are the only thing that matters* is sabotaging them and the people they interact with. You will be tempted, cajoled, wheedled, co-opted, and downright *pushed* to stray from the path.

You must reject the Lie and make a commitment to working from the truth:

It's not the results that matter.
It's your *actions* that matter.

Your actions are the part of the universal law you control. The part that leads to the result. The part that makes you a better manager. A better leader. A better collaborator. A better colleague, better parent, better spouse, better person.

This shift in focus from results to actions separates the professionals from the amateurs. The leaders from the tyrants. The managers from the controllers. Influencers from complainers. The behaviorally aware from the behaviorally blind.

In April 2018, I remember watching an episode of *American Idol* in which all the contestants were very nervous. Katy Perry, one of the judges, saw that it was affecting their performances. She told a contestant she was assessing, "Go back to your peers and tell them to forget the results. Just get out here and deliver." Katy's guidance was an attempt to shift the focus of the contestants from the desire to win (result), to the efforts required to deliver a winning performance (actions). And it worked. Nerves relaxed, and the quality of the performances improved.

Management has the potential to bring that same focus to the workplace. The focus that leads to satisfaction and gratification from delivering a better performance. And the focus that creates a meaningful impact on people and businesses.

Redirecting your efforts to the things that matter leaves people and places better than when you arrived. The actions that serve people best serve the organization best. These are actions rooted in integrity, respect, and inclusiveness for the long term. These are actions that support and guide, so we are all the better because of those actions, and we are all better off for what we have achieved together. *That's* leadership!

Be the leader who focuses on the things that matter, and you'll be the type of leader that makes a difference in people's lives.

ABOUT THE AUTHOR

Jim Vasconcellos has spent his career helping managers focus on the things that matter. He is an author, trainer, and professional speaker.

For over twenty years, he has been speaking about management and personal leadership throughout the United States, Canada, and Europe. And all this time, he's been listening to managers at every level, across a broad spectrum of industries. Each of these thousands of interactions has been a window into what works and what doesn't work for people and businesses trying to get things done.

Taking what he has learned, Jim has worked with companies and other organizations, instituting the principles to help people become the kind of manager that every business needs and every employee wants to work for.

QUESTIONS?
CONTACT JIM

jimv@resultsdontmatter.com

www.resultsdontmatter.com